Forward by Anc
Palmariellodivin

Andrew

When Barry emaile ...ᴗ ιᴗ write the foreword to this mighty tome, I was both honoured and mildly suspicious. Honoured, because Barry is a legend in our field. Suspicious, because I know what he's like and feared I might be unwittingly endorsing a collection of whimsical ramblings disguised as professional insight.

Barry and I go way back, over a decade of working together, exchanging ideas, and occasionally trying to outdo each other in the "who can be more sarcastic about Information Governance" stakes. He's always been the consummate professional: sharp, insightful, and generous with his time (especially when someone else's deadline is looming).

Now, about this book. At first glance, you might think it's just Barry letting off steam. And you'd be right, but only partly. Beneath the chuckles and occasional eyebrow-raises lies a rich vein of wisdom drawn from a career that spans several centuries (give or take). Barry's journey from RAF nurse to NHS Information Governance guru to independent consultant. and now, semi-retired raconteur, is all here, woven through reflections, many of which began life as LinkedIn posts and have now been lovingly curated into this collection.

Yes, some of these musings will make you laugh. Some might make you wince. And some will make you nod so vigorously you'll need a neck massage. But all of them are Barry through and through; thoughtful, provocative, and never afraid to say what everyone else is thinking (but wouldn't dare post online).

I've had the pleasure of co-presenting with Barry many times, and I can confirm he's a master of the unexpected tangent. Our carefully crafted scripts were merely suggestions to him, he preferred the scenic route, leaving me blinking like a rabbit in headlights while he riffed on the latest Information Governance absurdity.

So, thank you, Barry, for your wisdom, your wit, and your unwavering commitment to making Information Governance not just bearable, but actually enjoyable. And to Mrs M: may your patience be strong, your gin strong, and your tolerance for rants (that your favourite restaurant's Privacy Notice really shouldn't still mention the Data Protection Act 1998) be infinite.

Enjoy the read. You're in for a treat.

Andrew Harvey (Healthcare Information Governance Professional

Tania
It is a real privilege to write this foreword for my mentor, advocate, and friend, Barry J Moult.

I first met Barry as a young (yes I was once young but Barry seems to not have changed) and inexperienced IG coordinator who, like many, had “fallen” into the role. I had just been asked to lead on the IG Toolkit, full of enthusiasm but still finding my way.

At the East of England IG Forum, I met Malcolm and Barry — and the rest is history. From that moment, Barry set the standard. He made the complicated feel simple, the intimidating seem possible. His approach was always clear, concise, and pragmatic. No jargon, no ego — just solid wisdom delivered in a way that stuck. He never let us feel like imposters, always offering support and encouragement.

This book, *Things This Week*, captures exactly that spirit. It's Barry through and through: straightforward, practical, memorable. A true legend sharing his lessons in the way only he can.
With gratitude, memories of the laughter's and rolling eye moments
Tania Palmariellodiviney - Barry BEHAVE and I can see your eyes rolling

The look of disinterest, the look of despair, the look that says "please not GDPR"

I am a GEEK or depending on your age an ANORAK

Some of us just love our jobs, not because we know all the answers, but due to the variety and nuances that come with the job.

I was once asked "how would you sum up your job role?" I said you need to be a 'juggler', juggling several things each day.

In our jobs of Data Protection/Privacy/Information Governance no 2 days are the same. Question, challenges, changes in legislation and guidance. What you might have planned for the day, forget it, you may get to the end of the day and not touch any of the things you planned.

What also makes it fascinating is that colleagues from different sectors face the same question but from a different approach.

So how can we make of job roles interesting. In this short book I offer a light-hearted approach and a few serious items.

Please enjoy – I have included

1. Fun things to make the job interesting.
2. Some interesting things
3. Selection of "3 things this last week (from covid and lockdown

4. Colleagues. How they got into the DP/IG/Privacy sector.

Please add you own thoughts, additions, it is meant to be

light-hearted.

♡I love an acronym so sticking with ABC.

During training (mostly to the health sector) I remind staff that processing data for the delivery of '**direct health care'** the legal basis is ABC **'Anything But Consent'** (no doubt there are the odd occasion when it is consent).

1. Always Be Careful
2. Always Be Considerate
3. Anything But Consent
4. Always Be Compliant
5. Avoid Breach Chaos
6. Ask Before Copying
7. Anonymise Before Circulating
8. Always be clear
9. Assess Before Collecting
10. Avoid Blame Culture

New Year resolutions (when the new year comes)

1. Read ALL 99 Articles of EU GDPR (I dare you)
2. Reply to any ICO/Government consultations
3. Attend Privacy Space in April & November
4. Take on a DP/IG Apprentice (you know you should)
5. Launch a Privacy Awareness campaign that's interesting, informative and **FUN**
6. Carry out unannounced spot checks (managers will love you – NOT)

7. Carry out a ‘table top’ Incident response readiness.
8. Set up quarterly bring together IT, Cyber, AI, HR, Marketing and Comms
9. Push for policies to go beyond mere compliance
10. Subscribe to IRMS (or get the organisation to)

Why networks are important for DP/IG/Privacy colleagues

1. Meeting like minded colleagues

   A place to ‘sense check’ – I’m not going mad
2. Sharing best practice
3. Place to discuss difficult, complex issues
4. Confirmation that you are not alone
5. Discussing practical application of legislation and sector guidance (more practical than a book)
6. Find out what are the ‘emerging’ risks
7. Lessons to be learnt from others data breaches
8. Sharing policies and procedures
9. Different ways to deliver training
10. Learn about new jobs (don’t tell your boss)
11. Learn about new tech and tools

Driving a car….. Lessons for DP/IG or include in training and awareness

1. **Driving licence** to drive – Need a legal basis to process data
2. **Road signs** and highway code, know what they mean – UK GDPR Principle a guide to your journey
3. **Seat belt** to keep you safe – security measures to keep personal data safe & secure
4. **Dashboard** warning lights – Data Protection alerts when something goes wrong
5. **Speed limits**, stay within limits – Data Minimisation
6. **Google maps** or satnav, going from A to B – Know where your data is and where its going (no blind turns)
7. **Car Insurance** (risk assessment) – Prepare for the that incident, mitigate risk
8. **Passengers** – Data Subjects. You are responsible for their safety, rights and comfort
9. **Police** – Regulators enforcing the rules (maybe)
10. **Maintenance** – Ongoing compliance. Regular audits and updates

Secret Santa' – What can I get me colleagues

1. The Ultimate GDPR Practitioner GUIDE – Stephen Massey

2. GDPR for Dummies – Suzanne Dibble
3. Managing Subject Access Requests (practical handbook for every business) – Stephen Massey
4. Mastering AI – Nigel Gooding
5. Freedom of Information (A practical guidebook) – Martin Rosenbaum
6. Subscription to Amber Hawk course
7. Year membership to IRMS (little more expensive) but worth it.
8. Hoodie with a good logo
9. Mug with funny DP/IG saying
10. Pens with colleagues name on.

GDPR/DP/DPO/Privacy – ADVICE - Before you go on Annual Leave 5pm Friday

1. You will not have time to deal with the data breach that came in at 4.30pm – give it to someone else.
2. Put your email 'out of office' on – even better, send yourself pictures to fill up your email box (email not received mailbox full). (Deceitful but good)
3. DPIAs (note plural) that you haven't had time read and assess for risk…. Its ok, the Project Team informed you in plenty of time, another week will not matter. (As if)
4. Oh the DPIA for the new IT system that went live last week, and you were told about today – it can wait (it really can)

5. Cancel the training session – no one was coming anyway; they are on holiday and forgot to cancel. (Not the 1st time this has happened)
6. Be efficient, send apologies for the meetings in your calendar – not that you intended to go anyway. (Makes you look good)
7. Tell staff the things in the fridge belonging to you they can use – don't tell them its out of date today. (What a nice, kind and generous person you are (yeah right)
8. Empty your in and out tray so it looks like you dealt with everything before you went – even better hide the in-tray, (deceitful but good)
9. Leave a note on your desk with the word "passwords" and some random names and numbers. (They wouldn't, would they?)

GDPR/DP/IG Facts of Life.
The things mum and dad told you when you were 4

1. Learn about it early
2. It's not always nice
3. Everyone knows how to do it better
4. You will not find how to do it in a textbook
5. It comes naturally
6. Wish we had been told about it in school
7. Practice makes perfect
8. Men and women can do it
9. Sometimes it can be embarrassing
10. Sometimes you just don't feel like it

GDPR/DP/DPO/Privacy

Dealing with an email data breach – replies from famous catchphrases (see if you know the person who said it)

1. **"You stupid boy"** – on hearing an email was sent to wrong person
2. **"I don't believe it**" – On hearing they have done it a 2nd time
3. **"You plonker"** – On hearing they have done it a 3rd time
4. **"I have a cunning plan"** – to stop them doing it again
5. **"Am I bovvered"** – how I feel when I hear they have done it a 4th time
6. **"Just like that"** – showing them how not to send an email to the wrong person
7. **"Shut that door"** – on telling the person they are no longer required
8. **"Ooh Betty"** – on reporting the data breach to the ICO
9. **"don't panic"** – when you hear someone else has sent an email…. Guess where?
10. **"Is that your final answer"** – when you ask the CEO what he wants to do next

Give yourself an extra pat on the back if you know who said the catchphrases

GDPR/DP/Privacy – Athletics

1. **RUN** through your plan for the day to achieve your best
2. Compliance is a **MARATHON** not a sprint

3. There will be many **HURDLES** to get over
4. It's like a **PENTATHLON** with many and various things to do
5. **WALK** the walk – don't run
6. Remember to hand the **BATON** to other, it's not just your race
7. With some issues you will need to a **TRIPLE JUMPER**
8. Sometimes it like **SWIMMING** in deep water
9. At times it will be hard going to get to the **FINISH LINE**, don't give up
10. At times its right to be **PROUD** of your achievement

GDPR/DP/Privacy - Personal Ads.

1. **Experienced** - As old as Bazza. (Author of this book)
2. **Adventurous** - Been to Privacy Space. (See on LinkedIn)
3. **Sporty** - Runs around like a headless chicken.
4. **Professional** - Still wears suit, shirt & tie when on TEAMs & Zoom meetings
5. **Outgoing** - Never shuts up about GDPR (anorak – see comment later)
6. **Passionate** - Reads all the ICO guidance.
7. **Open minded** - Is like a dustbin, takes everything in (including snake oil from dodgy consultants on LinkedIn)

8. **Free spirit** - Claims your compliance ideas as their own.
9. **Contagious Smile** - When DPIA or RoPA is mentioned
10. **Good Communicator** - talks the talk but

Data Protection/Information Governance/Privacy- On the Job

a. **DPO** - Does it autonomously
b. **Senior Information Risk Owner** - Do it with reduced risk
c. **Caldicott Guardian** - Does it, but there's always a risk
d. **Chief Information Officer** - Does it in the 'cloud'
e. **CEO** - Tells others to do it
f. **Information Asset Owner** - Watches others do it
g. **Records Manager** - Makes sure its recorded when others do it
h. **Compliance Manager** - Makes sure others do it right
i. **FOI Manager** - Show others it's been done

Add other please (keep it clean)

10 things you NEVER hear Barry (the author) say:
(I've amended this since I've retired)

1. I'm not doing any more. (that is now only true-ish)
2. We are fully compliant. (ive never said that, never will)
3. I chose the wrong career. (I loved what I did 95% of the time)
4. The DSPT is my favourite. (no, I lie)
5. I'm taking August off. (maybe I took an odd day off)
6. I'm the best at planning. (If you know me, you know that's a lie as well)
7. I'm not coming to the Privacy Space (another lie – yes I am)
8. I'm never reading a Privacy Notice again (it's an addiction, so I will)
9. I'm not helping anyone again. (another lie… helped a few this week)
10. I'm supporting Arsenal (Son in Law hope you are read this) – (another lie – COYMP)

One-liners for GDPR/DP/DPO/Privacy

1. This is not my usual day rate - I'm on special offer this week.
2. I always intend to speak the truth about GDPR - so far so good.
3. I love DPOs - but I can't eat a whole one.
4. When I'm not in my right mind - I give my best advice.

5. For sale GDPR compliant software - used once.
6. I tried doing a DPIA once - it was a big risk.
7. A ROPA - is about as long as a piece of string.
8. Legal Basis to process data - have a guess.
9. Individual Rights - mind your own business.
10. Accountability – nah

I know - don't give up my day job.

10 reasons why it's great to work IGDP/GDPR

1. Because it matters… full stop
2. No 2 days are the same - never a boring day.
3. We know there are some awesome colleagues.
4. We have read all 99 Articles of GDPR - no one else has!!
5. We are the only people to read Privacy Policies/Notices - how cool is that?
6. Each week there is a new question we have not been asked before or considered - always a new challenge.
7. You don't need a degree - just passion, hard work and late nights.

8. You get to drink in the Privacy Office Arms with some real GEEKs (one day for real.... We promise)
9. No one fully understands your job - if they don't understand what you do, they can't get rid of you (unless they don't like you)
10. We know there is more than one answer to a question - the most popular answer is..... "It Depends"

GDPR/DP/IG/DPO.
Things written on the IG/DP/DPO office toilet wall. Not all has to be rude (keep it clean)

1. We must network sometime.
2. GDPR is a dirty word
3. Do you need training for this?
4. You will be pleased to know we can't charge.
5. We have you on camera (CCTV compliant) and we are audio recording you.
6. No need to flush we know when you have finished, we use AI
7. Do you have a legal basis to process that?
8. Before you start have you done a risk assessment?
9. You only have 1 Calendar month to comply.
10. Do you need the DPO for advice of what to do next?
11. Demonstrate compliance - Document Document Document but not on the wall

Someone mentioned the growth in acronyms
(Try working in health !)
Here are my GDPR acronyms

1. **DCWTL** - Demonstrate Compliance with The Law
2. **7P** - 7 Principles
3. **SLB** - Six Legal Basis
4. **YAOM** - You Are on Mute
5. **TYCO** - Turn You Camera On
6. **HTBR** - Has That Been Reported
7. **WAIT** - What Article Is That
8. **ID** - It Depends
9. **WDTGS** - What Does the Guidance Say
10. **BINL** - Because It's Not Legal
11. **CIGYACINA** - Can I Give You a Call I Need Advice
12. I**NTGAL** - I Need to Get a Life

What the Board wants to hear from DP/IG/Privacy/DPO Subject Matter Expert.

1. We take confidentiality seriously
2. All the Risks are covered
3. Thank them for their support
4. Tell them the Team is fully resourced
5. Show them a 'spiders web' and tell them data flows are covered
6. Tell them you don't want technology; you can manage with a spreadsheet
7. If anything goes wrong the DPO will go to prison as it's the only Mandated role

8 If we outsource IT. Security isn't our problem anymore
9 Accountability isn't the 7th GPRP Principle as there are only 6
10 We are FULLY GDPR compliant Seriously, when speaking to Board I will hang the washing on the 7th Principle

DPO 10 Commandments for Employer

1. You will not annoy your DPO
2. You will my comply with the law
3. You will have a legal basis for all processing of data
4. You will respect individual rights
5. You will complete all data flow mapping and record it in an information asset register
6. You will not only complete a DPIA, but you will also assess and mitigate any risks
7. You will learn all 7 GDPR principles off by heart
8. Your privacy notice will be up to date
9. You will provide your DPO with adequate resources
10. You will provide time & finance for your DPO to attend conferences and courses
11. Your DPO should be at a senior management level (paid appropriately)

DPO 10 Commandments (For the DPO)

1. You shall not be the fount of all knowledge (even if you are)
2. You shall be a facilitator not a hinderance.
3. You shall not quote GDPR articles to impress people
4. You shall not try to be clever at induction or mandatory training
5. You will answer your emails promptly
6. You will not moan at a Data Breach at 4.55pm on a Friday
7. You shall support staff and not criticise when they 'don't get it'
8. You will not 'chunter' in meetings
9. You will be always happy (GOOD LUCK)

You know you have been in the Privacy Office Arms or been to Privacy Space just a bit to long and had to much to drink. (Not me of course)

1. You think Richard Merrygold is handsome
2. You think Bazza is even more handsome
3. You think GDPR is sexy
4. You confess to knowing all 99 Articles
5. You suggest doing a tik-tok video (you really are drunk)
6. Everyone has left and you're talking about data breaches to the bar staff.
7. You can't remember your privacy from your protection from your infosec.

8. You keep calling Scott Salmon - Jeff.
9. You think a data flow is a map to your bedroom
10. Someone speaks to you, and you ask for their ID (sounds like US Police)
11. You can't understand why Gin/beer isn't a legal basis.
12. Why do people think you have a Pata Drotection problem, you don't have a Pata Drotection problem (I see your drunk again)

How you know you are a IG/DP/Privacy GEEK?

1. You always keep a pen and note pad by your bed for that 3am idea.
2. Your contact list is mostly other GEEKS (not exclusively)
3. When someone mentions a new company, you look up their privacy policy on their website.
4. Same as 3 but you look up their cookies policy.
5. If you are asked your name, address, DOB in a queue you whisper the reply.
6. You tut if people admit to having a Facebook account (even if you do)
7. You question why do they want ALL that information and where will it be stored?
8. You listen to webinars to see if the speaker is correct or to pinch their ideas.

9. You wonder if they do share your data even if they say they don't.
10. If I submit a SAR, will they give me all the info they hold?

Working from home. Love it or hate it – Advantages disadvantages.

- Tea/Coffee when I want.
- Breaks when I want.
- Dress how I want.
- No ties
- No Suits
- Shave when I want.
- Less petrol.
- Less car wear and tear.
- Car insurance down.
- A new one .... SLIPPERS.
- (I usually wore them for 4 hours a day and lasted about 4 years
- Now - worn 10/12 hours a day.... only last 1 year).

GDPR (Blind Date) Questions changed slightly

Q-What were you hoping for?
A-Something easy to understand and do.
Q-First impressions?
A-It's not that bad
Q-What did you say?
A-Who wrote this?

Q-Any awkward moments?
A-As DPO I will get paid more (wrong)
Q-Good parts.
A-Individual Rights
Q-Best thing about GDPR
A-Let me think
Q-Would you introduce GDPR to your friends?
A-Do I have a choice?
Q-Describe GDPR in three words?
A-Love Hate Relationship
Q-What do you think GDPR made of you?
A-Sucker
Q-Did you go on somewhere?
A-Nowhere to go... BAU
Q-If it weren't for GDPR, would you have a job?
A-Interesting thought
Q-If you could change one thing about GDPR what would it be?
A-Organisations to demonstrate they have considered correct resources.
Q-Marks out of 10 for GDPR
A-7
Q-Would you meet again?
A-Not me, I will retire.

You know when GDPR/DP/Privacy has got to you

1. You start making a list of things to do with GDPR/DP
2. You change the words of a song to put GDPR in
3. You write a new song about GDPR/DP
4. You order a coffee mug with GDPR/DP
5. Your screen saver is GDPR/DP

6. You put your GDPR Practitioner certificate on your LinkedIn profile
7. You only register for a webinar of its about GDPR
8. You think GDPR/DP is sexy
9. The only books you have purchased in last 7 years are about GDPR/DP
10. You don't get invited to a party/dinner because you will only talk about GDPR/DP

10 Things GDPR/DP/Privacy specialists say at work

1. I see your point bur GDPR/DP says no
2. I have plenty of ideals for compliance, but you will not like than
3. We would be better compliant if I had a more resources
4. A 20-page policy will be good
5. I have set time aside to do it, when? It Depends
6. I see we have another data breach on Friday
7. Of course, staff want to know when I'm doing a compliance audit

GDPR/DP/Privacy Geek, you know its about time you retired.

1. The 1st app you open at work is the SAGA app
2. Your unopened 'urgent' emails don't bother you
3. Your mid-morning coffee is now wine or gin

4. When someone calls you for a reality check you talk about your aches and pains
5. You need to look in your note pad to find your 4-digit pin to login to windows
6. You answer every question with 'it depends'
7. You start making promises you have no intention of keeping
8. When you learn more from your training than your delegates
9. You just add the next number to the end of your password
10. You spend more time reading the retirement policy that DP ones

In May, I was asked by a colleague who wants to get the messages of across to managers about their responsibility for GDPR.

Off the top of my head I said
Accountability
Principles or Policies
Record of Processing
Individual Rights
Legal Basis
That's not bad for April.

GDPR Principles by film titles (use your imagination) add to the list

1. **Lawful, Fair & Transparency**

Talk to Her. Total Recall. Back to the Future.

Transparency. Once upon a time in the west

2. **Purpose Limitation**

Purpose. A Dogs Purpose. It's Complicated. No Man's Land

3. **Data Minimisation**

Minority Report. Gone with the Wind. Out of Sight

4. **Accuracy**

To Have & Have Not. The Thin Red Line.
21 Grams. The Last Detail

5. **Storage Limitation**

Memento. Raiders of the Last Ark.
Gone with the Wind. Ice Age

6. **Integrity & Confidentiality**

As Good as it Gets. LA Confidential. Witness.
Tell No One. Titanic.

7. **Accountability**

Outside the Law. Kings Speech. The Usual Suspects.
Untouchables. The Great Escape

Which one is your favourite in each section?

Songs for Legal Basis of collecting and processing:

Consent

1 Voulez vous couchez avec moi?,
2 Consent – by Jack & Dean
3 Message in a bottle
4 Just need the green light
5 No Limit.
6 Would you go to bed with me
7 Hit me baby one more time.
8 I Do I Do – Abba

Contract

9 Sign Sealed Delivered,
10 Sign your name across my heart,
11 Signed sealed and delivered – Stevie Wonder

Legal Obligation

12 Breaking the law, Judas Priest.
13 I fought the law, and the law won - The Clash

Vital Interest

14 Heart stop a beat.
15 Live and let die Paul McCartney
16 Knocking on Heavens Door – by Bob Dylan or Guns and Roses

Public Interest

17 Look on the bright side of life.
18 Who shot the sheriff,
19 Arrest the president.
20 Take care

Legitimate Interest

21 9 to 5.
22 Great expectations

Feel free to add others

GDPR Individual Rights in song

1. **The right to be informed**
   - What's going on – by Marvin Gaye
2. **The right of access**
   - Gimme, Gimme Gimme – by Abba
3. **The right to rectification**
   - Changes – by David Bowie
4. **The right to erasure**

- Forget what I said – by the killers
- I want to break free – Queen

5. **The right to restrict processing**
    - Stop in the name of love – Supremes
    - Locked out of Heaven – by Bruno Mars
6. **The right to data portability**
    Wherever I lay my hat – by Paul Young
7. **The right to object**
    - Stop – by Spice Girls
8. **Rights in relation to automated decision making and profiling**.
    - Make up your mind – by Bucks Fizz

Songs for 7 GDPR principles *Lawfulness, fairness, and transparency*

a. Invisible man
b. Man in the mirror
c) I can see clearly now the rain has gone
d) It's no secret – by Kylie Minogue.
e) Man in the mirror
f) Invisible man.
g) Respect – by Aretha Franklin

Purpose limitation

h) Stop Right Now.
i) True by the Chain
j) Better the devil you know – by Kylie Minogue

Data minimisations

k) Leave your hat on by Tom Jones.
l) Enough is Enough
m) Someone watching me – Rockwell

Accuracy

n) Alright by E17.
o) True by the Chain
p) Can I find the right words – by Blonde

Storage limitation

q) Who wants to live forever – Queen

Integrity and confidentiality

r) Lost art of keeping a secret.

s) My lips are sealed Jim Reeves.

t) Jail House Rock

u) Safe and Sound – Capital Cities

Accountability

v) It wasn't me – by Shaggy

DP/GDPR Rules for work – Bazza's TOP TIPS

1. Apply common sense (let others complicate it, don't you)?
2. Don't keep quoting GDPR Articles (no ones interested in that, they just want to know what they can and can't do)
3. Make training interesting and engaging – use illustrations (real ones)
4. Reduce the size of your polices – If they are to long no one is going to read them or follow them.
5. If your DPIAs are 20 pages long, the Project Managers, Information Asset Owners are not going to complete it, or if they try then will do it badly.
6. Don't be afraid to ask questions, carry out due diligence
7. Don't be afraid to say NO or No until things change.
8. Make sure you have a good network – Imposter syndrome, 'brain fart' and need for reality checks

9. Your role is important, don't let anyone tell you it's only DP/GDPR'
10. Be willing to accept some risks – you can't remove all, but know what they are and record it

It's been said these words will be written on my 'tomb stone' – "Demonstrate compliance with the law" – Document, Document, Document. – Have I said Document?

Things you wish you could say at work.

1. I don't care what your excuse is ... but you will do a DPIA.
2. Yes, I could do the DPIA for you. But no, it's your job
3. I will reply to your email in 12 months' time, that's how long it takes you to reply.
4. Yes, it's a well set out policy, but I haven't a clue what it's on about, rewrite it.
5. I see a fairy elephant has been in the filing system.
6. You don't need to repeat yourself I got the impression you are stupid the 1st time you said it.
7. I'm imagining alphabet spaghetti making more sense.
8. Just because you use 100 words that no one understands doesn't make you a good boss.
9. No, I will not remove your name from the "you are a wally" list
10. Just go away you are ruining my day.

Principles be they GDPR x7 or in Health we have the Caldicott Principles x8. I've been thinking about DPO Principles.

DPO Principles

1. Understand current legislation, regulation, guidance and its application
2. Advice should be helpful, practical, and doable.
3. Training staff to know their responsibilities
4. Empowered to speak Up for the rights and freedoms of individuals.
5. Compliance should be monitored on a regular basis.
6. A good network with other DPO professionals is essential.
7. Balance between the needs of the individual and the organisation.
8. The Board/Senior Management should be regularly updated.

DPO moods you might be responsible for.

1. **Grumpy** - stop telling me GDPR doesn't apply to you.
2. **Sulky** - it's been one of those weeks, nothing has gone right.
3. **Happy** - Friday 5pm
4. **Angry** - When you tell me you have repeated the same data breach again.
5. **Cheerful** - When someone says the training was helpful.

6. **Reflective** - when I get a thank you.... doesn't happen often.
7. **Gloomy** - 8am Monday
8. **Humorous** - when I laugh at your stupidity.
9. **Melancholy** -
10. **Romantic** - when you get it right... I love you.

DPO/IG/DP

Work these out – give me a name (something to do with IG/DP/DPO)

- potted raincoat
- ammo centre's danger
- boat icy lunatic
- dividing hair lost
- bagels Lisa
- censors Fredric Pogo
- butters Jacques sec sec
- beer curtsy icy
- Francois immersions motion
- ache tabard

ANSWERS______________________________

6 Deadly terms used by the DPO (if you hear these words stop!)

1. **Fine** – the DPO is being sarcastic, it's not go ahead its fine.

2. **Nothing** – Is not a number but does relate to the number of times you have been told
3. **Go ahead** – The risk is yours (I wouldn't)
4. **Whatever** – Do it and the risk has just increased and so has the fine.
5. **That's Ok** – No it's not, the consequences are endless.
6. **Wow** – does not mean awesome, it means you are so stupid.

10 Fun facts

1 Project Managers (PMs) are there to annoy you

2 Stupid PMs annoy you even more

3 Project groups can't organise a booze up in a brewery

4 There is always one – and they work in your organisation

5 There's one born every minute – those born on 31st October 30 years ago are all in my organisation

6 The Policy that is most important is 3 years out of date

7 The new system that went wrong is the one someone said wasn't needed.

8 Data Breaches always happen on Friday afternoon

9 The Board member you need today is always on Annual leave TODAY

10 DPO is underpaid, undervalued and has the wrong line manger

DPOs report to the Board – when they found a compliance audit came back 85% compliant (using ICO compliance framework)

On completing the audit, I was:

1. Stunned
2. Startled
3. Taken aback
4. Stupefied
5. Confused
6. Shocked
7. Rattled
8. Dazed
9. Bewildered
10. Mixed Up
11. Surprised
12. Awed
13. Dumbfounded
14. Non-plus
15. Astounded

Hahahahaha I was dreaming. It might happen one day – just not today or a day this year or next

One of the questions I ask in a training session is "what do we see as emerging risks"

1. New IT systems
2. Increased use of Apps
3. Integrated Care Systems
4. A.I.
5. New legislation

6. Conflicting guidance
7. Cyber threat
8. Continued WFH
9. Lack of investment in IG
10. Lack of Subject Matter Experts (Recruitment)
11. Secondary use of data

Please add others.

Some things about the Data Security & Protection Toolkit (DSPT) for Health & Social Care.

1. Required to be completed by all delivering health & social care.
2. Been in place since 2003, originally called IGT and version 1 was just for Acute NHS Trusts.
3. Changed its name in 2018 to the DSPT and it became more technical focused.
4. Aim is to give assurance that data is being processed safely & securely.
5. There are 10 sections divided into 'assertions' previously called 'requirements'.
6. Some assertions are 'mandatory' others not.
7. To achieve 'standards met' all mandatory assertions will need to be completed.
8. There are 4 categories dependent on the organisation type.
9. Those completing and submitting the DSPT are seen as Trusted Partners for information sharing.
10. There is auditors' guidance for the DSPT, but auditor guidance asks for more than is required

in the DSPT.
11. Submission results can be seen by ICO, CQC, NHS and DoH.
12. DSPT has a breach reporting facility.
13. Completion of DSPT assertions can be allocated to different people in the organisation.
14. It is not meant to trip you up

Just had an interesting read about Larry Page of Google and Alphabet.
very interesting.

The name I knew and connection with Google, but not some of the other stuff about his life and health.

Another landmark tomorrow

(Tuesday) will be my last attendance at the National SIGN meeting (via TEAMs). I wish to thank all the past and present members of the group, for their help, support (including the time when I was chair). I can now spend time with my real job. There have been some great debates, discussions going back to the time of Phil Walker and Marie Greenfield, the IGA, and of course the IGT.
SIGN is in good hands with great Regional chairs and friend and colleague Andrew Harvey in the hot seat.

Today is East of England IG Forum. It is also my last as chair. (2018)
The forum started back in 2003/04 when the 1st

IG Toolkit was launched. The original forum was Myself, Michelle (Addenbrookes) Rees (Colchester) Gillian (Luton & Dunstable) and Chris from Peterborough. Without these the forum would not have existed. They allowed me to chair and have done so since those early days. The forum has grown and now has over 200 members, from all sectors in Health & Social Care (public & private). After today I hand over the reins to a new chair (to be elected). The forum has been a huge support to me and many others. I wish to thank everyone who is a member of the forum or has been for your input and support over the years.

This is a work issue (well accountancy one)
(I'm asking for a friend)
His mattress needs replacing, its effecting his sleep, therefore effecting his work. Can he claim the new mattress on expenses?
(Of course I'm asking for a friend)

Friends & Colleagues... I'm sure it's not just me (well I hope not).
If you are going to leave me (or anyone) a voicemail asking for me to call you back on a number .... **Please,** please, please (yes, I'm begging) state your number S-L-O-W-L-Y.

I've Just spent 10 mins repeating the voicemail 6 times and still got the number wrong.
If you don't state your number slowly, I'm not going to reply because I can't.

My Confidence ran away

I may come across as a very confident person, not fazed at challenging senior staff if required, or speaking at conference to people far more senior to me or answering questions on the spot. But this week I suffered a "crisis of confidence"

I was driving home from a conference I had spoken at. I reflected on the people there (very senior from Education), what I spoke about, my delivery.

Was it good enough? What did people think?
It felt heavy, dark... not sure how to explain it.
Panic, self-doubt...
Was I unwell - low blood sugar, tiredness, other issues? What was going on in my mind?
Do you have these thoughts? If so, you are not alone.
Weekend to reboot the brain cell, refresh, regain the confidence.
Stay safe friends.

Colleagues, friends, peers.... I need your help.

I'm struggling with the quote below. Am I miss reading it, getting the wrong end of the stick, not fully understood it? Or is it totally wrong??

This has stopped me having my Sunday afternoon nap.... I can't get it out of my mind. I must have read it over 50 times.
If I'm being thick, stupid, please be gentle when you tell me?

"If you process 'sensitive information' like race, ethnicity, political history, medical history, financial history or sexuality - you must first get user consent even if your processing falls under one of the 5 other legal basis"

As I consider the restrictions of summer 2020 and changes to how we work (new normal) and how it has affected me.

- No face-to-face training
- No exhibitions to attend
- The way we have dressed over the last 8 months.
- No suits
- No shirt & tie
- No shinny shoes

This week i reviewed my wardrobe.

- 7 suits
- 32 shirts
- 14 pair of trousers
- 64 ties!! (don't ask)

Question. How many of these are needed going forward?

- 2 suits
- 10 shirts
- 10 ties
- 1 pair of shinny shoes

Let's face it, it's not going to be the same, be it good or bad

Looks like I'm banning google maps from my car.

While driving this week for a few days' way with Mrs M. On a long straight road, I commented to Mrs M that it was probably a Roman road.
30 seconds later I get a commentary on Roman roads and other stuff (I was shocked) - maybe I shouldn't be.
Just to think of the things I've talked about when driving. (maybe about you the reader - it was all good stuff, honest)
What maps do people use? **Shhhh** someone is listening

How things have changed.

Since lockdown, I like many have been working from home.

- No trips to London to deliver training.
- No shirts, trousers, black shinny shoes, jacket (looking smart)
- Now its virtual training from home (Still trying to get used to it)
- Wearing shorts and smart casual polo shirt etc.

The point of this post. I've just noticed if got hair on my knees!!
Sorry ladies probably means nothing to you.

Telemedicine industry is worth about £20b, but It isn't new.

- 1876 - Graham Bell (I wonder when the 1st medical call was made?
- 1887 - H.R.Hertz. The 1st radio prog about health?
- 1925 - Dr Hugo Gernsback " teledactyl" (you will have to Google it)

- 1950. - 2 hospitals in Pennsylvania (24 miles apart) transmitted radiologic images via telephone.
- 1959 - Doctors in Nebraska transmitted neurological examinations to students.
- 2019 - very little had happened
- 2020 telemedicine arrives in the UK (covid consultations)

  11 **years of change in a few weeks !!**

  (OK slight exaggeration)

OK you old people in DP/IG/Privacy.

This week in a training session talking about Privacy Notices, I said only people in DP/IG/Privacy look at Privacy Notices because we are **'anoraks'** !!!

I got some funny looks from some of the younger folks ..... Why call yourselves “waterproof hoodies”?

(You oldies will understand the term **Anorak** !

How did you get into get into Information Governance/Data Protection?

Emma

My journey was a bit random. Did languages at uni, did a course to get a qualification to teach English as a foreign language, went to Italy, taught there for 2.5 years, came back, faffed about for a bit (including two stints waitressing and hotel work in California) trying to figure out what to do next, taught English to refugees in Salford, had enough of teaching, went to work for Plain English Campaign in the Peak District (key interview question: can you get here in the snow?). Was bored after a year and saw and an advert for the ICO in the Manchester Evening News. They wanted a range of people, across DP and FOI. No idea what any of it was but it sounded interesting. Got the role of head of international team in the policy dept and started what has turned into 16 years in data protection!!!

Amanda

I can't beat Emma's last story, but I spent 20 years in Pharma in Sales/Marketing and Medical. Because it's highly regulated, marketing 'within boundaries' was hard wired into me. While I was in the Medical Department, I used to approve all of the marketing materials with the ABPI in mind, and in another job, I used to run Clinical Trials. Long story but moved to Cornwall and had to wave goodbye to that part of my career, so took up with marketing local organisations - it made sense to me that there

are regulations outside Pharma too, and with that in mind, I 'found' Data Protection. Did the CIPP/E and a Post Grad Cert along with a couple of fab study buddies H and T.
The way I look at it - growing a business is like driving a car. You need an accelerator (marketing) and a brake (Data Protection) to keep the car safe. Sometimes all it needs is a tap on the brake as you whizz along, but other times, it's a full-on EMERGENCY STOP

Derek

I went from policing to management consulting with EY and Capita as a contractor, then into the security sector. I took a diploma in security management, and I submitted one module on

the up-and-coming GDPR. Went to work in Bosnia consulting on security for the State Prosecutors Office, met with the Ministry of Security there and got into security of classified data. Fast forward to the end of that contract and decided to put my experiences and (then) recent training in GDPR to use. Started my company and away I went!

Tash

Mine's not interesting enough: I got a job to do open-source software compliance but there were too many GDPR clients stacked up, so I had to do that instead. My journey to data is slightly more interesting; I thought I was interview for a sex phone line job (I was desperate for a job) but it ended up being a job in one of Wales first call centres updating corporate information

Ben

Went from working in a nightclub while studying and trying to get work in music industry (worked for free in a local recording studio a few times), to working in a Tribunal Centre updating case records while trying to make it as a football coach (did level 2 coaching badges while playing semi-pro level), to working in Ministry of Justice (MoJ) private office managing ministerial correspondence where I encountered FOI for the first time. That's when I got interested and moved into MoJ's central team that managed FOI and SARs and ran training on both FOI and DPA. The rest is history I guess, went to Kings College London to manage FOI/DPA for the uni and work with the NHS trusts and various research teams, then PwC in my first data protection only role and then back to public sector at Homes England as DPO. Not sure if that's interesting or not. Used to have Hens drink a cocktail from a glass wedged into my trousers, though not sure how that helped to become a DPO. Risk management maybe?!

Claire

I was a solicitor working in a corporate law firm specialising in Environmental Law. I was obsessed by Civil Liberties when I was a law student but couldn't really see a career path in that, so sort of went with the money and a

traditional route. I had a miscarriage and was a bit broken so chucked the towel in!!! (Still can't believe I did that looking back). Then did a few project management roles but didn't really stick at anything. Then retrained as a volunteer counsellor (en route to a counselling career), was enjoying it but somewhat impulsively applied for a job as a School Business Manager (I was a Brownie leader so did a bit of finance, safeguarding and organised trips). Then someone spotted me because I was emailing the council with lots of questions about the GDPR and suggested I should answer those questions from inside the council! Completely love it and found my passion in life- it's very similar to my work as an environment lawyer- bit of contracts, bit of EU regulations, a government regulator so a bit of enforcement, bit of litigation... with counselling, project management, knowledge of how schools work,
safeguarding and civil liberties thrown in for good measure.

Richard
The lady who was Information Governance Manager needed an assistant. Apparently, she also had a penchant for young men. 3 interviewed, I got the job…that was 12 years ago

Terry
Army
Fire Service PRO to Fire Service - Project Manager (National IT Project - when the Govt. of

the day declared all LA services will be delivered electronically- never worked out how to get water through an RJ45 connection). My first involvement with DPA. Then to Fire Service FOI manager and first got qualified in DP (ISEB Cert.). NHS IG Manager (Contracting resulting in 75% pay increase).NHS to telecoms company (wider InfoSec remit), then back to health care (charity sector IG Manager again), then managing InfoSec consulting team delivering services to corporate clients. On to the Financial Sector for a couple of years before a short break to obtain CIPP/e, then moving on to Retail (back to my passion of predominantly DP - but still with wider IS and PCI-DSS throw in).Finally, and hopefully remaining in Logistics focusing purely on GDPR/DPA.

Debbie

I started at the Crown Post Offices after I was kicked out of (sorry, suggested I leave) the WRAF for daring to marry someone in the ranks (I was one of the youngest to get my commission in the WRAF at the time). That didn't last long (the marriage) so I moved and worked as a secretary in a HGV garage (interesting posters back then) and as a licensing officer for a small council, inspecting and licencing sex shops amongst other licence work.

I retrained in IT as a programmer (this was the mid-80s when I was told I could earn more sitting at my desk). Them were the days, no PCs and what were laptops?

I moved back up t'north eventually, contracting

as a programmer.
I was learning to fly when my flying club asked me to become the manager. Took a 50% pay cut and did that for 2 years before being made redundant.
Had to go back into IT in local government around 1990.
Was asked if I could cover Data Protection (yep, the 1984 Act) and have done so ever since around other roles in local gov (programming, IT Trainer, Corporate Info Manager, and IG Manager with sole responsibility for all Info Law).
Implemented 1998 Act, FOI, EIR, RIPA, GDPR and 2018 Act, and then got told by my new director that I didn't have experience to be their DPO so I left (more to that story).
And here I am now.

Selection of my 3 things this week. (as posted on LinkedIn). Insight into the work and thoughts of a DPO

3 things this week. (1)

1. I attended a local football club this week
Adults £10
Concessions £7 (Result for me).
Concessions please I asked.
Your joking pal. (He then asked me for ID to prove in was entitled to a concession).
Like what I said?
Driving licence !!
No I said. He was not getting any ID from me. (Actually, I didn't have any on me)
After a stand-off.... he clicked the gate and let me in.
Don't mess with seniors 😛

2. I managed to visit a hospice this week where I'm the DPO and carried out an audit (nothing huge) but enough to challenge them. They have a very active IG Steering group. They are enthusiastic to get things right.
I'm the DPO for 5 hospices the engagement from all 5 is commendable.

3. I attended the West Suffolk Business Award evening last night Friday (Black tie) I tell you, I scrub up tidy. I was not up for an award, but I was privileged to see and hear some award winners, truly inspirational individuals, and companies. Just think what more could be achieved with more investment. Thank you to Alex Till (Menta) for the invite and Claire

Brooks for looking after me. Great company, great event.... but Bazza didn't get home until after midnight

3 things this week. (2)

1. This week it's not just a shout out to a colleague or organisations I work with, but my greatest support.... yes Mrs M. There was good reason for me to cancel some meetings this week and spend time at home, but she insisted I continued and not let people down.

Some of you know why and thank you for your comments.

2. Having been a Governor at a local hospital and having to stand down last December. I became a Governor at our local primary school a year ago. On Monday at the Governors meeting the chair stood down!!! I now find myself having to stand in to be chair (not by choice). Education is a new field to me but looking forward to the challenge.
I have some good support from the local authority. If any of you have any advice - please DM me.

3. Now to work. My colleague Tania Palmariellodiviney (MSc) and I have been working on supporting a local authority completing a DPIA. Having a colleague bringing an extra pair of eyes and new perspective on the risks is so good. At times we need a reality check. We may be good or ok at our DPO jobs

but having good colleagues and network is important.
Looking forward to the 'DPO Reset' next month. (Extended pub chat).

3 things this week. (3)

1. My week consisted of (a) DPIA training for HC-UK Ltd (b) SIRO training for DPAS® (c) Intro to the new DPOaaS E&NH GP Practices (d) Demo of redaction software by Folding Space (e) UK GDPR training update for staff at HBL ICT - Partnership in IT (f) Education project for Luton Borough Council. Pub Chat (virtual) with Andrew Harvey LLM for Robert MBA, CIGO, CIP, IGP InfoGov World Magazine. Plus numerous TEAMs calls.
I'm so pleased to have Tania Palmariellodiviney (MSc) working with me and keeping me sane. Busy week but very rewarding.

2. I visited some of the GP Practices I'm DPO for. GP Practices are doing a great job (I'm not looking for a debate). One issue that came up in all of them was SAR. On returning home I saw a post on Twitter by a very respected colleague who pointed out some very poor practice by a local hospital. I agree the process was not helpful at all. I was then made aware of someone just wanting the results of one single test. (Again, the process not being helpful.

SAR does not need to be this painful, bureaucratic, and unhelpful. Yes, it does need to be right. To be honest i was embarrassed.

Clear training guidance needed.
3. Those of us who work in health, the wheels of change are already happening, pre the Health & Care Bill passing through Parliament, House of Lords before receiving Royal Assent. Out go CCGs and in comes Integrated Care Boards. Here we go again change, and BAU.
Life is never dull in the world IG in Health.

3 Things this week. (4)

1. I have been doing FOI since its introduction in 2005. I've been challenged and questioned. I've done internal reviews. What I've never done is apply a vexatious request, I've been close, this week I've been as close as I've ever been... but I stepped back.

2. I'm almost ready with a book for my IG/DPOs friends and colleagues in time for Christmas. I was inspired to do it by a LinkedIn connection who said DPOs are hard to buy for apparently.

3. I thought we had seen the end of Privacy Notices quoting DPA 1998 (but no) I've had 3 this week. I also had one that said GDPR replaced Data Protection 1998. I know the only people that look at them are us 'anoraks' but come on orgs get it right, please.

Have a good and safe long weekend. Plus, its match day

3 things this week. (5)

1. Garmin or Google maps?

I have both, but I find Google maps better.
I am used to it giving instructions, but yesterday I asked Mrs M a question and it I got a reply "I didn't understand that". Not from Mrs M but from Google maps. That is not the 1st time, last time was when I mentioned a Roman Road and Google started to tell us about Roman Roads in the UK. The rest of the journey was in silence from me and Mrs M.

2. I've been contacted 4 times this week by colleagues enquiring about the DP/IG Apprenticeship, who are looking to recruit. Hold on just a little while longer. The good news its making great progress, and official announcement should be forth coming in the next couple of months. So excited.

3. We're all going on a summer holiday, no more working for a week or two (oldies will understand). Please don't let your security guard down... actors out there looking to hack your systems

3 Things this week. (6)

1. Face2Face IG training at a hospital .... yes real, real people.
It was so good to be out of the house and to stand before NHS staff. I didn't wear suit or tie, just smart casual. Mask when walking from A to B, but off when training. After 15 months I thought it would be difficult, I didn't need to worry, all went well.

2. Watch this space. In the next few weeks, I hope to announce the name of a IG colleague I've known and respected for over 15 years who will joining me as an associate to deliver some bespoke IG/DPO work. It's not who you think (now that confused you) .... it is ......HER name to be announced very soon.
very exciting times.

3. This week it was the closing date for Health & Social Care orgs to submit their DSP Toolkit. Many of you may have read my friend & colleague Andrew Harvey LLM Post about his masters dissertation on the DSPT.
What does the future hold for the DSPT?
Is it just a 'pain'?
Does it fulfil a purpose?
Does it give assurance you are handling patient data safely?
Has it become a tick box exercise?
Is it to big?
How can it be changed to make it of value?
Answer to those questions are out of my hands.
Personally I think it could be changed to make it easier to complete and still fulfil a genuine purpose.

Have a good weekend & stay safe

3 things this week. (7)
1. The big ticket item, the GP Patient data extract. It has now hit national and local press and TV. On the 1st of July NHSD proposes to download your GP data for the purposes of research and planning. By the 23rd of June you

need to have registered you opt out. There are many issues with this, not least that patients have not been informed sufficiently to make an informed decision.
If you are not up to speed Google it, look at twitter and LinkedIn posts. It does affect you.
I hear as of yesterday it is going to be challenged in court to either stop it or delay it.
Life is never dull in the NHS IG world.

2. Email data breaches and phishing scams.
My message is
a) for emails is
Pause for 3 seconds before hitting send. Check you have the right recipients.
Check you have the right attachment.
a) For phishing scams.
It only takes 1 click
Stop
Think
Report

If anyone is good at doing posters for either of those ☺ let me know.

3. I had to attend a store to purchase something. When paying I was asked for my email address for the receipt to be emailed to me. (I know its old hat now) what did surprise me is when I refused, a conversation pursued the attendant told me he gets £5 for every new email address he gets. Wow !!!

3 Things this week. (8)

1. I had a call this week from friend/colleague

(SC) who has just been made redundant. I was gutted for him. If I see a job posted on LI, I share it, or if I see people have lost their jobs, I share it in the hope it might help. #SHARE

2. Following @Privacy Space event on Thursday in the discussion room 'Security Knowledge'. Is there a need for a:
IT Security for DPO Dummies? I know my job in Data Privacy/Protection but Changing the password on my router !!! #HELP

3. DSPT Audits
Following a conversation this week It was confirmed what I already knew ... internal audits ask for evidence beyond what is required for the DSPT. It puts additional, unwarranted pressure on staff. #STOPIT

3 things this week. (9)

1. Careful what you say. There is a world of difference between dulux paint and 'durex' paint (if there is such a thing). What's worst the Freudian slip you have made? (The above was not me)

2. Following a SAR when there is still a difference between the requestor and the organisation. When there is very little that can be done but refer the requester to the ICO. Maybe we don't want to do that. I would rather work with the requestor to come to a solution, but that is

not always possible.

3. The other big thing this week was the DPPC2021. This was the 1st virtual ICO conference with over 3000 able to attend. The technology worked well. Maybe some of the content, speakers could have been better. Although there may be a place for virtual, it does not replace the F2F network, meal and drink with colleagues.
Will be interesting to see what happens over the next 12 months.

3 Things this week. (10)

1. Following last week's Line of Duty episode and now the classic one liner "Jesus, Mary, Joseph and the wee baby donkey"
I've been thinking what my classic one liner might be. It will have to be **"demonstrate compliance with the law"**
What's your best work onliner?

2. I chaired an online conference this week about demonstrating compliance with GDPR for HC-UK Ltd . If you have not heard Andrew Latham of Capsticks talking about Duty of Candour, you should. If you get the opportunity, take it.

3. I made a mistake this week (I probably make many) thankfully not huge, just silly, and stupid. Is it natural to start to look for excuses, to blame

technology or pressure of work, even the excuse "everyone makes mistakes" ?   My best excuse "must be my age"

3 things this week (11)

1. During a training session I made a huge mistake. I used a wrong word in describing a scenario That wrong word changed the discussion and outcome. I didn't realise what I had done. It trying to explain it, I made it worse. Lesson to me. Be more careful and shut up !!

2. Respect does not always need to be earned ... it should be part of human life. I saw a YouTube video talk by a military officer. He said: "If you can't treat someone with dignity and respect.... get out"

3. On reviewing a privacy notice (PN) on a health organisations website, I clicked onto the one at the bottom of the website page. It was not the orgs PN but the website developers. The health org did not know they needed their own for their service users. Still work to be done out there.

3 things this week (12)

1. I watched a video this week on YouTube. '5 silly questions women should not ask their husbands'. I think we are all guilty of asking silly questions in our work. Is it to make us feel

superior or to belittle someone? Stop it !!

2. I was asked the other day who in 'work' has been the biggest help and support over the last 20 years?
IG Managers (Mel & Jodie)
SIROs (Craig and Dawn)
CGs (Pam, Dermot and Angela)
COO (Gwen)
Health Records Manager (Helen)
6 of those were Directors.
1 of then trusted me to be a Snr Manager on Call, they probably don't realise what that meant to me.
3 of them I line managed, but they not only supported me they challenged me and made me better at my job.
To all (and the many others) THANK YOU.

3 things this week. (13)
1. I often say, "ask 10 Info Gov professionals the same question you will get 10 different answers" The same can be true if you post a comment here on LinkedIn !! (#JustSaying)

2. I had a LinkedIn message from someone I didn't know. The person wanted to 'bounce' a dilemma they had. I listened, we discussed, and said our goodbyes. I don't know what decision they made. Sometimes we all need help/advice, a place to discuss issues, to help inform our

decisions. It's good to talk.

3. SAR in health can be very complex. Can we disclose and should we disclose? Maybe legally yes, but ethically, morally, should we?
Every case will be slightly different, with a different answer. My advice. Seek advice from different sources to inform your decision, and document document (did I say document) your reason & rationale for disclosure.

3 Things this week. (14)

1. When me role as a DPO in reviewing DPIAs, Policies, Privacy Notices impacts my personal life. I have been looking at comments about a local planning application. I find myself pulling it apart. Questions not answered, ambiguous statements and researching other planning application for consistency!!! SAD

2. Today is International Happy Day. I want to be happy every day and make people happy everyday.... BE HAPPY 😊

3. This week I've been asked to do something I've not been asked before...I never even thought about it, it wasn't a 'thing' for me.
I can't write a book, (I don't have the skills) but what about being asked to write a 'forward' for one. I'm honoured to be asked. HAPPY
Stay Safe, Be Kind, Be Happy

3 things this week (15)

1. I attended a virtual meeting this week, which started at top of the hour. Over the next 45 minutes people kept joining the meeting. One joining just as we were finishing. Being ex Forces I learnt from that turning up on time was essential. (Now I know that there are times when delays can't be helped and its out of your hands, I understand that). Do we now except that late arrival is acceptable? Should there be a cut off time i.e 5 or 10 mins after the meeting has started and you will not be allowed in? (unless you have notified the organiser prior to the meeting). Maybe its my age (GOMS)

2. I realised this week, we need to be clear what we mean when using terms and phrases, it might be clear to me and you, but not others and certainly not those new in our profession. Definitions are important.

3. I will leave with this quote "If someone treats you bad, just remember that there is something wrong with them, not you. Normal people don't go around destroying other people". Yes, it happened

3 Things this week. (16)

1. I'm part of a local businesses Zoom meet on Tuesdays. Its for SMEs. They are keen to do

things right, even with the Data Protection stuff. One business contracted a website developer. They asked the developer about a Privacy Policy. The developers said they had one they could put on the webpage. The local business took the developers word that it was appropriate. Why would the local business know if it was appropriate or not? I wonder how many local businesses are in this position and need support? In this case my support.

2. This week (more than before) I've been contacted by friends and ex colleagues looking to change jobs. They feel they don't have the traction with their organisations anymore, or it was down to internal politics. Do they tough it out, or change organisation? Difficult decision. This is why I passionately believe support groups are vital. You are not alone. Don't be alone.

3. Not everyone comments on LinkedIn posts. When I comment, it is from my experience, in the health sector. It is not meant to be a definitive answer, but just my opinion. Hopefully, it will help to inform others to make an informed decision from the replies they receive. I value your opinion.

Stay Safe and have the jab

3 Things this week. (17)

1. I'm part of a local businesses Zoom meet on Tuesdays. Its for SMEs. They are keen to do things right, even with the Data Protection stuff. One business contracted a website developer. They asked the developer about a Privacy Policy. The developers said they had one they could put on the webpage. The local business took the developers word that it was appropriate. Why would the local business know if it was appropriate or not? I wonder how many local businesses are in this position and need support? In this case my support.

2. This week (more than before) I've been contacted by friends and ex colleagues looking to change jobs. They feel they don't have the traction with their organisations anymore, or it was down to internal politics. Do they tough it out, or change organisation? Difficult decision. Therefore, I passionately believe support groups are vital. You are not alone. Don't be alone.

3. Not everyone comments on LI posts. When I comment, it is from my experience, in the health sector. It is not meant to be a definitive answer, but just my opinion. Hopefully, it will help to inform others to make an informed decision from the replies they receive. I value your opinion.

Stay Safe and have the jab

3 things this week. (18)

1. I'm on a number of discussion sites for colleagues working in GDPR/DP/IG
#LinkedIn
#Slack
#Watercooler (google and have a look)
To me they are a lifesaver, somewhere I can go to get a 'sense check', also to contribute to questions asked by others. They are safe places and not a place for criticism. Never too old to learn.

2. Problem with my email for 3 days earlier this week. It even kept me up at till midnight with a call to a service desk. I'm still not sure if emails I sent were delivered or if you sent one to me. Sorry if I've not replied. Good news is that at 9pm Friday I started to receive emails from Monday & Tuesday. It might have been quicker by old fashioned letter this week. Technology is great when it works, frustrating when it doesn't.

3. I was delivering training on DPIAs Friday (virtual). I really enjoyed it. Was it down to me? NO. It was the engagement of attendees (16 in total)
All cameras on, lots of questions, engaging discussion. Please remember it's not just down to the trainer... but the attendees as well, that could be me and you. We are all still getting used to virtual training, which is here to stay for some, but I'm looking forward to face2face at some time. #HC-U

Have a good weekend, get your jab

when offered and stay safe

3 things this week (19)

1. This week I made comment on a process flow chart. WOW it caused some debate.
Maybe I should not have said anything, but I did. Good debate can help refine what we think and do. We can have different opinions; we can learn from one another. Even I'm not too old to learn. Thank you for your comments and opinions.

2. As you know I'm passionate about IG. I want people see it as a career choice. Hence, I'm involved in the Apprenticeship Trailblazer group looking to get an Apprenticeship standard approved. Also, I've been asking that in the NHS IG has a A4C profile. This is important step to recognise IG as a profession.

3. A question I get on every training course I take. EU/UK Data Protection Adequacy Agreement. 86 pages long, 285 items.... someone must feel proud this weekend that it's now been presented as a draft, ready to be ratified. Good luck reading it. I'm waiting for others to summarise it 😀🤪

The sun is shining, it warm...🌞 enjoy the

weekend.
Stay Safe

3 Things this week (20)

1. I have a family member asking for some IG help. As this is a new clinical service they will be providing, they will have to complete a DPIA, RoPA, register with the ICO and will need to complete the DSPT as the work will be commissioned via the CCG. As a clinician they were surprised what must be done in the background. Maybe there needs to be some comms to explain what the role of IG is and how it links with clinical work, to keep patient data safe and secure.

2. I've realised how important it is to have trusted colleagues who you can contact when you need a reality check. I'm also on a couple of secure social media groups (safe space) to share thoughts and advise. It's also invaluable to have colleagues in fast dial.

3. Those of us working in Health & Social Care we could be in for another change. (Nothing new there). I hear a rumour that the Govt is considering new legislation to give more power to the SoS for Health for the delivery of care through the NHS. So, it will it be a repealing of the H&SC Act 2012 and replacing it with a new Act? I smile because it seems (for those of us

who have been around for a while) we might be back to 'Health Authorities' (but called something else)
Call me cynical 😊

3 things this week (21)

1. Imposter Syndrome. Been a real issue for me this week. It's really and difficult to deal with. It took just one negative comment !!!

2. This week I've been trying to work out how best to do RoPA in a practical way that will be done and kept up to date and will not be unreasonably resource intensive.
I work with some Health organisation who have a large number (hundreds) of data flows, internal and external.
If it's too complicated, time consuming it's unlikely to be completed and kept up to date.
Who should be completing them IAO?
Even software as good as they maybe take time to complete. (Yes, there are some good products on the market).
Am I alone in these thoughts?

3. Today is DELETE WhatsApp day. I now have Signal.

3 things this week (22)

1. This week I've made comment on 2 pieces of

draft guidance. Both documents were biased and in one case totally advocating a conflict of interest. Both documents IMHO demean the role of my colleagues working in Information Governance in Health & Social Care. My colleagues deserve better. I hope those issuing the guidance reflect on what they have publish and making radical changes or withdraw the guidance.

2. I had a conversation with someone regarding a SAR. I wanted some clarification as it was complex request. I didn't want to apply an extension, so was looking to help them.
I was told I was not under any circumstances to apply any redactions. Really??

3. I have had a conversation with a colleague thinking how we could help small local charities on a voluntary basis, who are struggling with DP/UK GDPR. Some who have nothing in place or if they do its totally inadequate.

3 things this week (23)

1. It would be wrong not to mention Google v Lloyd. (If it doesn't mean anything to you, you need to Google it or maybe some other browser that doesn't drop cookies)
As someone said Google won, and the compensation chasers lost.
The case was based on the DPA1998, would GDPR have made much difference? IMHO no, but maybe the lawyers would have a different

opinion. Is this issue/debate dead? I doubt it.

2. Life has its ups and downs. This week has been such a week. The funeral of my mother-in-law. She was 95 and right up to her death she kept her sense of humour. For the last 3 years she has been cared for by Barchester Healthcare

They have been amazing. Thank you to Amy and the staff at the Spires in Lichfield. Sometimes it's not always about work.

3. Thursday and Friday saw me in London for the DPO Reset. I was staying at the Union Jack Club. As it was 11/11 the club was full of service and ex-service people who have served their country in the Armed Forces.

We thank them for their service and sacrifice. #Remember

As for the day with other DPOs, I was privileged to be with such people, not only their knowledge, expertise but also their good humour (they put up with an 'oldie') Make sure you have a network of like-minded colleagues. BTW, Covent Garden is looking very festive!!!

3 things this week (24)

1. In a few weeks it will be Christmas, New Year and my Birthday. As the new year approaches, I need to review my own business strategy for the coming year. (One year at a time). It will include present business, new business, attendance at

conferences, exhibitions... but I'm also making sure that the strategy includes downtime for family, holidays. (When you work for yourself, those things are part of business)

2. I've not strayed into commenting on the Pandemic in my '3 things this week'. This week 2 grandkids (age 8 and 6) and my daughter in law have tested positive. It's not a problem as they have been reasonably well with it. How much different it has been for others, being very unwell, admitted into hospital and sadly some people still dying. Please be careful, stay safe. Coronavirus has not gone away.

3. After 3 postponements the IRMS - Information and Records Management Society Conference is taking place, starting next weekend. Looks like another 'pub chat' presentation with Andrew Harvey FIRMS, LLM, EU-GDPR-P . (We should have patented it when we 1st did it pre GDPR)
If you are going please stop and say hi, even if we have not chatted before (call it care for the elderly)

You may not be able to attend the conference this time, but they are playing catch up with one next year. But it's not just about conferences, being a member has many benefits and resources and membership is not expensive.

Help
I'm being dragged out shopping today 🥴
wish me luck.

Some random comments

I was asked on Tuesday why I attend events like Privsec?
Number of reasons

1. Because I can. I'm the boss.
2. I'm a people person. I love being with people.
3. The networking with other Privacy colleagues.
4. An interest in the presentations.
5. Meeting new and old vendors/sponsors.

If I was to pick just 2 (nothing against the others) Zivver would be one for their secure email and the fact they don't hold the encryption key.
Facit Data Systems I just loved their CCTV system, and pixelated images.

oh and coffee, cake and a beer

Attending PrivSec I was introduced to someone as being 'the godfather of privacy'
Not sure if that was reference to my longevity in the work OR my age 🥴
Thinking about it both could be true. Looking around yesterday I think the later may well be truer.
Next time someone will get slapped with my pension book 🤪
I'm looking forward to attending next year, if they let old men in 😀

Dilemma. We usual give our children and grandchildren a Christmas stocking on Christmas Day.
It usually contains small novelty items, many would be plastic and wrapped in plastic. We have been asked not to this year to cut down on the use of plastic. We totally agree with this. BUT something families have done for generations. We are going to embrace the request. Yes they will be getting the Christmas stocking, but greater thought at what they will contain.
#COP26
#environment
#ChangingHabits

How embarrassing !!
Do any of my consultant colleagues running their own business, registered with Companies House know what Companies House Act 2006 s82 says?

I was caught out, I was not fully compliant (only about 75%), I had some but not all, and was an oversight on my part (I could blame 2 others for not telling me what I needed to do).
Basically I had something missing on my website and email.
I have now rectified the 'error' and all is good. It took less than a minute, literally !!

Having had the non-compliance pointed out to me, I did a little bit of due diligence. (Looked at some of your websites and emails you have sent me. Well done to those who are compliant, BUT there were a significant number that were not....

join the list of bad boys and girls with me. The fine for non-compliance is £1000

This is what s82 says:
In accordance with s.82 Companies Act 2006, all companies must disclose –
1. the part of the United Kingdom in which the company is registered;
2. the company's registered number;
3. the address of the company's registered office;
On all:-
(a) its business letters;
(b) its order forms; and
(c) its e-mails
(d) websites.

Please shout out if you are super good or wish to thank me for saving you a few hundred ££

Just a thought.

If Facebook are thinking of rebranding (I suggest it's called FaceLift)
Will WhatsApp be rebranded and called 'WhatsAface'?
Will Instagram be rebranding and called 'Instaface'?

getting my coat.. .

Just an observation

Interesting observation today at the HETT in ExCel and National Cyber at Olympia. Exhibitors on their stands who sit or stand and talk amongst themselves while I (and others) walked by...

stopping and looking at their stand and they don't engage !! (not all the exhibitors were that bad) but many were. They pay good money to be there.
Maybe they need training on how to be an exhibitor making the most of the opportunity.

Hints & Tips

I have read several articles/posts about the important things to succeed in the Privacy sector. Not that I disagree with them, several things can help an individual move forward in their careers.

As many will know, I do not come with a raft of qualifications in Privacy/Data Protection. My early years education was very limited, due to social background, and my interests in football and girls (I wasn't successful with either).

My career in nursing was a key factor, giving me an understanding in personal and sensitive data.

Each one of us is different, in our likes and dislikes, things that motivate us, even in our jobs, what is expected of use within our job description, the people we work with, and the support we get. Even our location can play a big part, due to the availability of job opportunities. (Recent moves to hybrid working have made location less of a problem).

So here are my tips to develop a successful career in Privacy.

1. Don't be afraid to start at the bottom and work your way up. You will learn the nuts and bolts of the job. Get your hands dirty by doing the job.

2. Be practical in your advice. It must work, or people will not do it, or if it's too long and complicated.

3. Don't just attend meetings, listening is not the same as hearing what is being said. Make notes and evaluate after.

4. Choose the courses you do carefully. It's not just a case of lots of letters after your name. Remember there are varying aspects to the job role. You need courses that are informative, practical and will help you do the job now and advance your career.

5. Attend conferences, with good speakers. Sometimes a 30 min presentation can be as informative as a half day training course.

6. Attend webinars (choose carefully). These too can bring great learning from experts in their chosen subjects, with lots of useful takeaways.

7. Find a job (not always easy) that will give you the potential to grow.

8. Network. Don't just be parochial, look further afield. Find networks that will help, not hinder your development.

9. Find a few privacy professionals that you trust, who you can go to for help, advice and support. (ask them to be your mentor), sometimes a shoulder to cry on.

10. In work, don't sit behind a desk all day. If you are physically in work, instead of answering an email with an email…go visit them in their office. If working from home, arrange a TEAMs met.

11. Get involved in workshops. Your input and opinion as a junior is important, as it will help others to understand.

12. Don't be afraid to say NO or admit you don't know something. Ask for support.

13. Attend Exhibitions (again choose carefully) Speak to the Vendors/Suppliers. Find out what they have to offer.

14. Learn from your mistakes. Review and evaluate what you have done, so that lessons can be learnt.

15. Have a sense of humour. Learn to laugh at yourself.

16. Show passion, enthusiasm and love for the job you do.

17. When training, be engaging… tell a story

The Silent Death by Policy

We're all familiar with the infamous phrase "death by PowerPoint, " but let's shine a spotlight on another critical issue that often flies under the radar: "death by policy"

For years, I've emphasised during my training sessions that policies are not mere guidelines—they are essential "must do" and "must not do" directives for staff. Why? Because when a serious data breach occurs, regulatory bodies like the Information Commissioner's Office (ICO) demand copies of relevant policies. These documents serve as a litmus test to determine what staff members were informed about.

Policies play a crucial role in assessing whether an organisation had the necessary "organisational measures in place" (including procedures, training, and other safeguards).

But it doesn't stop there. The impact of policies extends beyond data breaches. Consider HR and disciplinary matters: Which policies did a staff member fail to comply with?

These questions underscore the significance of robust policy implementation and enforcement.

So, let's not underestimate the power of policies—they're not just words on paper; they're the guardians of organisational integrity.

PURPOSE

Why do we need a particular policy? What do we include to make sure this aim is met?

"Words carry power. Choose them wisely"

While this phrase can really be applied to any situation, it is doubly true when creating policies as, in essence, that is all they are comprised of. Like a poet, we need to take extra care in how we want to carry a message across, and how we can do so in the most concise way with the most impact.

"Consistency is key"

Years ago, I faced a surprising situation. I received a Freedom of Information (FOI) request for copies of corporate and department policies. As I collated them, I was taken aback—they looked as if they had been written by different organisations. There was no consistency in format or layout.

How can we expect our staff to align their practices with the policies when we're unable to align the policies with each other? It's confusing and draining for staff and simply put, bad practice.

Consistency is key in ensuring policies are read, understood and applied appropriately.

REVIEW

Are our policies being followed? Have they, perhaps, become outdated? Do they work?

You want me to read ALL OF THAT!?

A 30-page policy might seem a brilliant idea if we are only considering what content it's meant to cover, but this falls short extremely quickly once we must account for who's meant to read it. No one wants to read and memorise a drawn-out document, it's simply a mundane and monotonous chore.

Have we made this clear to you?

We know why we have our policies, but do we know if they're being followed? There are many ways to monitor this, but we don't want to act as babysitters when doing so. We want capable staff, not mindless robots who do our every bidding. Regular, but not constant, auditing and checks of staff practice in relation to our policies help us gauge not only staff's understanding of policies, but also any areas of confusion or vagueness within the policy that we can address.

It's time for a change...

Organisations are constantly subject to major changes, whether it's the law, our team members or even our practices. We can't, however, let ourselves become victims of these changes and must take the reins. We must be prepared to address any new considerations that may arise and update our policies promptly and accordingly.

SIGNING OFF

Actions we can employ to ensure a standardised approach not just in developing policies, but in signing them off as well.

Far too often, I encounter policies within organisations that lack any formal check or sign-off process. To address this, I propose the

establishment of a 'policy review committee'. Their role isn't to create policies but to meticulously scrutinise them once they've been reviewed and updated. Here are the critical questions this committee should ask:

Correct Emphasis: Does the policy convey the appropriate level of emphasis? Consider replacing vague terms like "should" with the stronger "must".

Layout Consistency: Is the policy formatted correctly, adhering to the agreed-upon structure? Uniformity in layout matters.

Consistency Across Policies: Does the policy align with other existing policies? Inconsistencies confuse staff and lead to divergent practices.

Timely Updates: Has the policy been recently updated? Ensure a new review date is added to keep it current Clarity and Precision: Is the policy clear and concise? Avoid unnecessary duplication. Staff engagement improves when policies are succinct.

Compliance Monitoring: How will compliance be monitored? Regular checks are essential. When was the last assessment carried out? Once the thorough review is complete, the policy returns to the owner for final sign-off by the organisational manager, relevant department head, or an appropriate committee. With this process in place, the policy is ready for dissemination across the entire organisation.

REMEMBER!

Well-crafted policies are the backbone of organisational clarity and consistency!

Policies are the compass guiding organisations through the compliance maze!

Well-structured policies are the bedrock of organisational effectiveness

Do not let your organisation be a victim of Death by Policy

The Silent Death by Training

Is Data Protection/Information Governance/cyber/AI Governance Training important?

YES – it's part of your UK GDPR compliance *"…. §organisational measures in place"*

Are you guilty of causing 'Death by Training?

We have heard it said, or feedback says:

Repetitive - same as last time
Boring – not relevant, no passion
Not applicable – does not apply to my job role
Uninspiring – Speaker had no passion for the subject

To long – could have been done in half the time
Didn't understand it – to many acronyms

Training needs to be relevant to those attending, not repetitive.

How long should training need to take?

Depending on the subject and those attending.

30 min, 1 hour, 2 hours, half day, full day, 12 months

Think about the subject and the audience and content to be delivered. Is it an overview, is to a focused topic? Is it detailed?

Training can be longer i.e. DP/IG Apprenticeship 18 Months. DP/IG Practitioner Course 5 months (with tutor sessions, assignments, and exams). Half day and full day courses (or even longer)

Delivery of training.

People learn and respond to different delivery methods.

- Face 2 Face
- Online with tutor
- Videos
- Tabletop exercises
- Scenario sessions
- Modulor training
- Games

You will not please everyone, but think about what will work best for you and those attending (even a mix of the above)

What training needs to be delivered and how often

- Induction training – Monthly (dependent on the organisation)
- Mandatory Annual training – Annual (as required by any regulators)
- Specialist training – As required (dependent on the job role i.e. Cyber)
- Department Training (dependent of data they process)
- Board Training – Annual (issues relevant at the time)

Have you carried out a Training needs Analysis?

Who delivers the training – Internal (who is best placed?)

Data Protection/Information Governance Lead
Data Protection Officer
Risk Manager
Department Manager
Information Asset Owners (Data Protection Champions)
Head of Cyber/IT
How engaging, up to date, relevant, inspiring are they?

Does your organisation use external trainers?

Training companies/Consultancy
Subject matter experts
Is it 'certified' i.e. BSC
Is it value for money?

Have you evaluated the training, (internal or external) and seen it with your own eyes and ears?

Training isn't a 'tick box' it is part of your compliance ".... organisational measures"

Training needs to be:
Engaging
Inspiring
Up to date
Relevant

Fun

Don't cause Death by Training – it could cost you

SAR - ICO

Bristol City Council are not the 1st to be mentioned in dispatches by the ICO for SARs delays, they will not be the last.

There are several issues why organisations struggle (not just Bristol City Council) - not in any order (and there may be other causes)

1. Poor Process organisations did not review the process for several years (we have always done it this way)

2. Training of staff dealing with SARs. Mostly junior staff and not seen as a priority.

3. Training of staff who may hold the data in their departments (let's call them IAO)

4. Investment in software (not always the answer but can help in logging requests and redaction)

5. Recruitment. Staff with relevant skills (not necessarily experience), they can be trained.

6. Lack of Snr Management accountability (not in every organisation). They do not have eyes on governance reports.

7. Finance There is a financial squeeze on most public bodies. Dilemma - Children's Services or SARs??

8. Substantial increase in requests.

To every problem there may be a solution (organisation need to think about priorities and risks) - I'm not suggesting its easy.

Sometimes it's looking for Support maybe externally.

(I'm not suggesting me - give me a break, (I'm retired). But I am available to give advice and point to those who can help and support.
Including:
Data Privacy Simplified Ltd
iSTORM® Privacy - Security - Pentesting Consultancy
DPAS® Tash Whitaker

Friends that is it. The END

Whatever you do remember these 3 things

1. Document, Document, Document
2. BEHAVE
3. Tim Turner gave me a badge earlier this year (2025) at Privacy Space. “Retired but not Retiring”. That’s me.

Printed in Dunstable, United Kingdom

70615400R00050